The Bill of Rights
Fifth Amendment: The Right to Fairness

by Rich Smith

Series Consultant: Scott Harr, J.D. Criminal Justice
Department Chair, Concordia University St. Paul

VISIT US AT
WWW.ABDOPUBLISHING.COM

Published by ABDO Publishing Company, 8000 West 78th Street, Suite 310, Edina, MN 55439.
Copyright ©2008 by Abdo Consulting Group, Inc. International copyrights reserved in all countries.
No part of this book may be reproduced in any form without written permission from the publisher.
Abdo & Daughters™ is a trademark and logo of ABDO Publishing Company.

Printed in the United States.

Editor: John Hamilton
Graphic Design: John Hamilton
Cover Design: Neil Klinepier
Cover Illustration: Getty Images
Interior Photos and Illustrations: p 1 Constitution & flag, iStockphoto; p 5 angry mom and boy, Getty Images; p 7 Constitution & quill pen, iStockphoto; p 9 lawyers argue before judge, Getty Images; p 11 lawyer presents evidence, Getty Images; p 13 officer making arrest, Getty Images; p 14 officer holds up Miranda warning card, AP Images; p 15 woman in back of squad car, Getty Images; p 17 suspect being interrogated, Getty Images; p 19 officer questioning man, Getty Images; p 21 men testifying, AP Images; p 23 lawyer consulting with client, Getty Images; p 25 John Revelli, AP Images; p 26 Bryon Athenian in front of New London house, Getty Images; p 29 scales and gavel in front of flag, iStockphoto.

Library of Congress Cataloging-in-Publication Data

Smith, Rich, 1954-
   Fifth Amendment : the right to fairness / Rich Smith.
      p. cm. -- (The Bill of Rights)
   Includes index.
   ISBN 978-1-59928-917-5
   1. Due process of law--United States--Juvenile literature. 2. Right to counsel--United States--Juvenile literature. 3. Grand jury--United States--Juvenile literature. 4. Double jeopardy--United States--Juvenile literature. 5. United States. Constitution. 5th Amendment--Juvenile literature. I. Title.

KF4765.Z9S65 2008
347.73'5--dc22
                        2007014575

CONTENTS

INTRODUCTION

Maybe this has happened to you: You spend your Saturday at the mall, buying some clothes, watching a movie, having some fun with friends. Then you come home. You notice right away that something is missing from your room. You realize that your entire collection of comic books has disappeared.

Twenty boxes full of comics you've been hanging onto since you were old enough to read are gone. Twenty boxes containing all your favorites, everything from rare first-issues to the comics that came out just last month.

Who would do such a rotten thing to you? Who would take belongings of yours without even asking?

The first thing you do is wonder if the comic book thief is someone who lives in your home. Maybe it was your kid brother. He's been known to do sneaky things, including stealing your stuff.

So you burst into your brother's bedroom and tell him you know he stole your comic book collection. He denies it. You tell him again you know he's guilty. He again insists he's innocent. You threaten to make big trouble for him if he doesn't confess to his crime. He starts crying because you don't believe that he's telling the truth.

Now you're really mad. You shove him into his closet and lean up against the outside of the closed door so he can't open it and get free. He pounds on the door and begs to be let out. You tell him you'll only let him out if he admits he stole your comic book collection. Your kid brother is very afraid of the dark in the closet. He cries out, "Yes! Yes, I stole your comic books. Now please let me out."

You open the door. Your kid brother is standing there with tears streaming down his face. You say to him, "OK, I've let you out. Now give me back my comic books."

Just then, your mother comes into the room, unaware of what you had done to your brother. She only heard the part about him needing to give you back your comics. She explains that he can't give them back to you because he did not take them. You ask your mom if she knows who did. She says *she* did. She threw them all away when she cleaned your room while you were off at the mall. She did it to make space for a study table she wants to put in your room. She understands that you might not be too happy about her throwing away your boxes of comic books, but she says you'll get over it. Besides, those comic books weren't worth anything, she says. You, of course, know they were worth a lot. But your mom doesn't care.

Below: If your mom has ever thrown away your comic book collection without first asking your permission, then due process, or basic fairness, was violated.

Has your parent or guardian ever done something inconsiderate like that to you? If so, then you were denied your right of due process.

And you in turn have denied your younger sibling his or her right of due process if you've ever forced a confession for a bad deed he or she did not do.

You can see why no one should ever be denied the right of due process. That's what the Founding Fathers of the United States believed. They felt due process was so important that they made sure to include it in the Constitution's Bill of Rights.

That right is specifically mentioned in the Fifth Amendment. Here is what that amendment declares:

"No person shall be held to answer for a capital, or otherwise infamous crime, unless on a presentment or indictment of a Grand Jury, except in cases arising in the land or naval forces, or in the Militia, when in actual service in time of War or public danger; nor shall any person be subject for the same offense to be twice put in jeopardy of life or limb; nor shall be compelled in any criminal case to be a witness against himself, nor be deprived of life, liberty, or property, without due process of law; nor shall private property be taken for public use, without just compensation."

The words used by the Founding Fathers in describing your due process rights are very formal and very old fashioned. That's because they were written more than 200 years ago. The style of writing is very different from today's way of writing. That makes the Fifth Amendment difficult to understand. But don't feel bad if you have trouble understanding it. Lots and lots of people have been arguing over the meaning of those words for a very long time now.

Still, there is one thing most everyone can agree on: The Fifth Amendment is all about fairness.

Above: A replica of the United States Constitution.

What Is Due Process?

The United States Constitution is a document that describes how the U.S. government is set up and operated. It also explains the job of the president, the lawmakers of Congress, and the people who work as judges. At the end of the Constitution are 27 additional instructions for the government. These are called amendments. The first 10 make up what is known as the Bill of Rights. The Bill of Rights lists the special freedoms every human is born with and is able to enjoy in America. Also, the Bill of Rights tells the government that it cannot stop people from fully using and enjoying those freedoms unless the government has an extremely good reason for doing so. Included in the Bill of Rights is an amendment that defines due process: the Fifth Amendment.

Everybody in the United States is guaranteed the right of due process. It doesn't matter if you were born here or are an immigrant. It doesn't matter what ethnic group you belong to. It doesn't matter if you're male or female, adult or child. It doesn't matter what your sexual preference is. It doesn't matter if you have a disability. According to the Fifth Amendment, everybody in America has the right of due process.

The purpose of due process is to make sure that government behaves in a fair and honorable way when it tries to put a person in prison or take away his or her property. Government is responsible for getting criminals off the streets and for helping communities to become better places to live. The Fifth Amendment requires that anything the government does in the name of public safety or progress be done the right way.

Due process comes in two flavors. One is called *procedural* due process. The other is *substantive* due process.

Procedural due process is about the rules or procedures the government must follow when taking action against you. Having government obey rules is extremely important. It is how fairness is guaranteed. Freedom is lost any time government fails to follow the rules.

The rules government must obey under due process are many. They were created by Congress and expanded by the Supreme Court. Most were a result of complaints from people who had been treated unfairly by the government.

Substantive due process is all about making sure the government does not have one set of rules when it acts against you and then a different set when dealing with other people. Substantive due process means the rules government follows must work the exact same for you as they do for everyone else. For example, it would be a violation of substantive due process if the government were to pass a law requiring African Americans who use public buses to sit all the way in the back and leave the seats in the front for whites only.

Below: The Fifth Amendment was written to assure that the government acts fairly when it tries to punish people or make them do something.

STRIKE UP THE GRAND

A JURY IS A GROUP of ordinary people from all walks of life who make decisions based on evidence presented to them. The juries you are most likely familiar with are known as *petit* juries. These usually have from 9 to 12 people, and meet in a courtroom. Their job is to decide on the guilt or innocence of individuals accused of lawbreaking.

Another type of jury is the *grand* jury. This is a group of 12 to 23 people. A grand jury decides whether there is enough evidence against a suspected lawbreaker to have a court trial with a petit jury. Grand juries are the type talked about in the Fifth Amendment.

The importance of grand juries is that they help make sure prosecutors act honestly and fairly when building a case against someone they accuse of the most serious types of crimes. This helps protect against out-of-control prosecutors trying to send innocent people to prison.

A grand jury that believes there is enough evidence for a court trial writes up a list of charges against the accused. These charges are called indictments. In some situations, they are called presentments.

Among the evidence a grand jury may consider is testimony from the accused person. However, the accused has a Fifth Amendment right to not answer the grand jury's questions if he feels his testimony would get him in more trouble than he already is in.

Evidence brought before a grand jury is almost always presented in secret. The Supreme Court long ago decided that grand jury secrecy is constitutional. However, secrecy is one of many complaints people have about grand juries. Another complaint is that the accused cannot have an attorney present. Also, the accused are not allowed to call witnesses to help in their defense, and are not allowed to hear the testimony of the prosecution's witnesses.

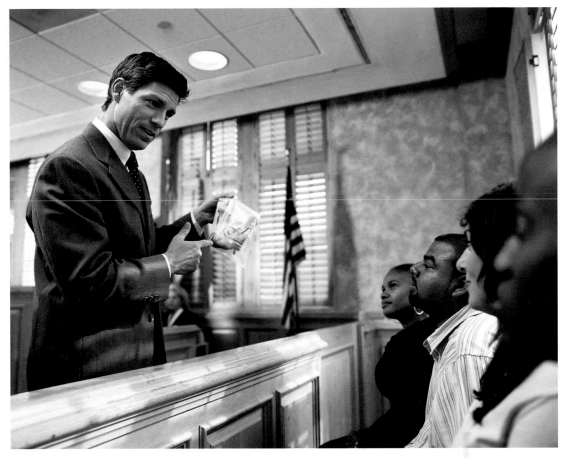

These complaints have convinced many states, counties, and cities to stop using grand juries. They have replaced grand juries with a system they believe is more fair and efficient. It is known as the preliminary hearing. Preliminary hearings are conducted by judges. Prosecutors tell a judge why they believe there is enough evidence against an accused person to win a conviction. The accused, along with his or her attorney, then has a chance to point out all the weaknesses of the prosecutor's evidence, and explain why it would be a waste of time to take the case to trial.

The judge listens to both sides. If he or she agrees with the prosecutor, a date is scheduled for a full, formal trial of the accused. If instead the judge agrees with the accused, the charges are dropped and the person is free to go.

Above: A lawyer presents a piece of evidence to a jury. A petite jury works in a regular courtroom, and has 9 to 12 people. A grand jury usually has from 12 to 23 members, and meets in secret.

MIRANDA RIGHTS

Nearly every cops-and-bad-guys TV show or movie you've watched has a scene in it where the police finally catch the villain they've been chasing. This scene usually includes the heroes slapping handcuffs on the villain and declaring, with great satisfaction, these words: "You have the right to remain silent. Anything you say can and will be used against you in a court of law. You have the right to an attorney present during questioning. If you cannot afford an attorney, one will be appointed for you."

You've probably heard these lines enough times that you can recite them from memory. But these words are spoken not just by Hollywood actors and actresses playing police officers. They are spoken hundreds of times each day in cities and towns all across America whenever real-life police arrest and question someone concerning a serious crime.

Saying these words is known as reading crime suspects their rights. Which rights? The rights guaranteed by the Fifth Amendment, which include the right to fair treatment while in the hands of the police and the right of people not to be witnesses against themselves.

The requirement that police read these rights to an arrested suspect comes from a 1966 United States Supreme Court case known as *Miranda v. Arizona*. The case began with the conviction of a man named Ernesto Miranda, who had been charged with kidnapping and rape. The Arizona police who arrested Miranda asked him many questions about the two crimes. They wanted to know where he was at the time the crimes took place, and if he had been involved. Miranda gave answers that made himself look guilty. In fact, the more the police questioned him, the guiltier Miranda seemed. Finally, Miranda realized there was no point in any longer claiming to be innocent. So he confessed.

Above: When police arrest people and ask them questions, they must explain to the suspects their constitutional right to not be a witness against themselves, and their right to talk to a lawyer.

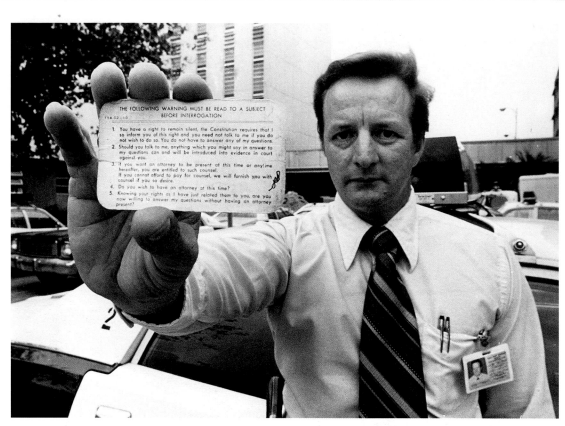

Above: An officer with the Miami Police Department, in Miami, Florida, displays a card that is often used by officers to read a Miranda warning to crime suspects.

Miranda's confession to the police made it easy for the prosecutor to win a conviction against him in court. All that the prosecutor needed to do was show the jury Miranda's confession. No witnesses to testify against him were even necessary.

However, Miranda's attorney thought this was all very unfair. In appealing the verdict of guilt, the attorney argued that the prosecutor should not have been allowed to offer Miranda's confession as evidence against him. First, he said, Miranda was never told by the police that the Fifth Amendment's protection against self-incrimination gave him the right to remain silent during the time they were asking him questions. Also, the attorney said that Miranda was never told by police that the Fifth Amendment's due process clause meant he could have had an attorney with him during that questioning.

The Supreme Court agreed with Miranda's lawyer. The Court ruled that Miranda clearly did not know what his rights were. Police and the prosecutor used Miranda's lack of knowledge to gain an unfair advantage over him, the Court decided.

Included in the Court's *Miranda* ruling were instructions to police and prosecutors all over the country that suspects held in custody must be told about their Constitutional rights before questioning begins. The Court did not tell police exactly what they had to say when reading suspects their rights. However, the Court in the years since then did offer helpful pointers.

One of those pointers is that the police must explain Fifth Amendment rights in a way that will be understood by the person they've arrested. That is why police officers usually end their reading of the suspect's rights by asking if he or she understands. That is also why translators are always used to explain these rights if the suspect mainly speaks a language other than English.

In some states, laws have been written that require police to ask not only if suspects understand their rights, but also if they are willing to *waive*, or give up, the right to remain silent and be questioned with an attorney present.

Above: A police officer advises a suspect of her Miranda rights.

Forced Confessions Are Not Allowed

Having rights read before the start of police questioning is known as giving an arrested suspect the Miranda warning. Police often refer to it as "Mirandizing" the person they have in custody. A criminal trial becomes more difficult for prosecutors to win if police fail to give the Miranda warning when required. If police gather evidence as a result of questioning a suspect who hasn't been Mirandized, that evidence is usually not allowed in court.

Of course, this is all very different from the way questioning was handled in the time before the United States became a country. Centuries ago, especially in dictatorships, authorities could legally threaten to kill your family, burn down your house, and take away everything you owned unless you agreed to admit your guilt. You would have to confess even if you weren't guilty of anything and could prove your innocence.

Authorities were allowed to use torture to make you confess. Sometimes this meant keeping you awake for many days and never letting you sleep. Other times they beat you up with their fists and with big wooden clubs, or they splashed you with boiling-hot oil. A few people were able to withstand these terrible acts. For them, the authorities brought out the really evil tools of torture. One was an expandable rack. The victim would be laid upon two overlapping planks of wood with his hands tied to the end of one plank and his feet bound to the end of the other. Machinery would then pull the two planks away from the overlapping center. The person's body would be stretched as a result.

And it would keep being stretched until there was so much pain that the victim begged for it to stop. But to stop the torture, the person first had to agree to admit to the crime the authorities said he had committed.

Confessions made because of threats or because of torture were in those days allowed as evidence that could be used in court. It was not until shortly before the U.S. was created from the 13 British colonies that England made it illegal to use such confessions, which are called *coerced confessions*.

However, coerced confessions did not entirely disappear after the United States became a country. They were used by many local U.S. police departments during the 19th century and well into the middle of the 20th century. It was not until the police grew tired of having the Supreme Court constantly set free people who had made forced admissions of guilt that they finally quit using coerced confessions.

Above: Admissions of guilt obtained by threats or torture are called coerced confessions.

WHEN IS A MIRANDA WARNING REQUIRED?

A MIRANDA WARNING is given to anyone taken into police custody on suspicion of committing a serious crime. The warning must be given before police begin questioning the person they have taken into custody.

Being in police custody usually means the person is under arrest. But it also can mean the person is merely in handcuffs and not yet formally under arrest. It is considered being in custody if the police have someone in a place or situation where they are not free to walk away, and would have no reasonable reason to think that they can.

The Miranda warning is given so that people in custody will know they have a Fifth Amendment right to say nothing at all to the police. It is also given to remind people they have a Fifth Amendment right to have an attorney who can help answer questions from the police. Attorneys can step in to stop the accused from accidentally saying something that will later hurt them in court.

An arrested person is free to speak to police and answer their questions after receiving the Miranda warning. But whatever the person says from that moment forward can be used against him or her in court.

It's possible for an arrested person to make a full confession before receiving a Miranda warning. If so, he or she cannot later claim the confession to be unconstitutional. That's because the confession was given without the police having asked any questions. A Miranda warning is only necessary if police are going to question the person in their custody.

Another situation where no Miranda warning would be needed is if a person walked into a police station and confessed to a crime. He could not later argue that the confession was unconstitutional. The reason is that he was not in custody at the time he gave the confession.

Above: After being given a Miranda warning, suspects may answer questions asked by the police, but anything suspects say may later be used against them in court.

"I TAKE THE FIFTH"

The idea behind the Miranda warning comes from the Fifth Amendment's guarantee that nobody can be forced to testify against themselves, which is also known as *self-incrimination*. A series of decisions by the Supreme Court since the 1920s made it clear that people have the right not to self-incriminate, whether they are being tried for serious crimes or being sued for money by neighbors. It doesn't matter if the trial takes place in a federal court or one that is operated by a state, county, or city. The right to not self-incriminate is promised just about anywhere that a person might be asked to testify to tell the truth, the whole truth, and nothing but the truth.

Someone who stands on his or her right to avoid self-incrimination is said in street language to be "taking the Fifth," or "pleading the Fifth." Many people declared "I take the Fifth" during the 1940s and 1950s, when Congress conducted hearings into the activities of organized-crime gangs. Mobsters were questioned by senators and members of the House of Representatives about horrible crimes that had been committed in Chicago, New York, and other big cities around the country. But the gangland thugs repeatedly refused to answer on the grounds that doing so might lead to their arrest for having been involved in the very crimes being discussed.

"I plead the Fifth" was also a frequent response of a few people from Hollywood, California, who were asked by Congress about Communists working in the movie industry. In the years right after World War II, Americans worried that the former Soviet Union was plotting to take over the United States. Indeed, congressional committees had received information that the Soviet plot included using movies to corrupt the morals of Americans so that they would become too weak to resist the Communist-led nation. Some of the film directors, screenwriters, and celebrities who testified before these committees had past links to American Communist groups. They refused to answer

questions about their involvement with those organizations. The lawmakers responded by finding these Fifth Amendment pleaders to be in contempt of Congress. That upset many people because the Hollywood testifiers were given a punishment just for having exercised their constitutional rights.

Something similar happened about 15 years later to a man named Mr. Griffin who refused to answer questions under oath in a California courtroom, where he was on trial for murder. The prosecutor told the jury that Griffin certainly had the right to plead the Fifth and say nothing. But then he added that the jurors should take his refusal to answer as proof of his guilt. If he were innocent, he would have nothing to hide, the prosecutor claimed. That made sense to the jury, so they found Griffin guilty of first-degree murder.

Griffin appealed the verdict. In 1965, the U.S. Supreme Court ruled in *Griffin v. California* that it was unfair of the prosecutor to have portrayed Griffin as guilty just for using his Constitutional rights. The Court then reversed the trial court verdict against Griffin.

Above: On August 31, 1961, two men rumored to be members of an organized crime gang testified before the Senate Investigations Subcommittee in Washington, D.C. The men invoked the Fifth Amendment in refusing to answer questions about their business or occupations.

ONCE IS MORE THAN ENOUGH

Another important right written into the Fifth Amendment is the guarantee against being put on trial two or more times for the same crime. Leaders of the very young United States remembered how the British courts sometimes used a technique called *double jeopardy*. This was a way to put people in prison after having been found innocent of whatever law they were accused of breaking. It worked like this: The government charged people with a crime and tried them in court. If they were found not guilty, the government kept charging them with that same crime over and over until they were finally found guilty. Double jeopardy was a fearsome tool for getting rid of law-abiding people whose opinions the government didn't like. Just the threat of double jeopardy being used was enough to make people promise to do anything the government wanted.

People in the United States are very happy that they do not face double jeopardy when they are taken to court. However, no right is absolute, not even the right against double jeopardy. In fact, there are situations where the government can try a defendant two different times for the same crime. For example, a person accused of committing a hate crime can be tried in federal court and then again in a state court. The Supreme Court has ruled that this does not count as double jeopardy, since the federal government and the state government are really two separate governments.

Another situation where a person can be tried twice is when a judge has been paid money or some other type of bribe in exchange for finding the defendant guilty or innocent. That's a phony trial, which doesn't count. The accused must go through a new trial with an honest judge. But this new trial will count as the first time he or she is tried.

Something similar happens if there is a mistrial. This usually occurs because of some kind of procedural error by the judge or lawyers. This forces a stop to the trial before the jury can weigh the evidence and decide on the guilt or innocence of the accused. Then, at a later date, the accused can be put on trial again for that same crime. This is not double jeopardy because the first trial technically never happened.

It is also not double jeopardy if the accused is tried in criminal court and then later in civil court. In 1995, NFL Hall-of-Famer O.J. Simpson was accused of murdering his wife and her friend. A jury cleared him of all charges, and he walked out of the Los Angeles, California, criminal courthouse a free man. But then the relatives of the murder victims sued Simpson in civil court for wrongfully causing those deaths. The civil court jury found Simpson guilty. Civil courts do not have the power to put people in jail for wrongful deaths. They punish the guilty by making them pay money to the people who sued. In this case, Simpson was ordered to pay the relatives more than $33 million in damages.

Below: A lawyer consults with her client in a courtroom.

No Taking Without Paying

The Constitution describes how the U.S. government is to be set up and operated. It also explains the various jobs of the government. One of these jobs is to help America make progress toward a better life for all. There are several ways government can do that. Among the most basic is by building roads and bridges so that food, products, and people can easily be transported to wherever in the country they are needed. Free movement of people and goods helps the economy grow. A growing economy allows for greater and greater prosperity shared by more and more people.

But in order for there to be roads and bridges, the government must first have possession of the land on which those things will be constructed. Let's say there is a city that wants to build a superhighway from its factory district all the way to the gigantic shopping mall in the center of another city. The problem is that a farmer owns all the land between the two cities and refuses to let a superhighway be built through it.

In the days before the Bill of Rights, the government could solve the problem by simply grabbing from this farmer whatever amount of land it wanted. It wouldn't have to ask. It wouldn't have to beg. It wouldn't even have to pay the owner money to make up for the land that was taken.

Thankfully, the Fifth Amendment forbids this sort of government unfairness. Yes, the government can still take someone's land for a road or bridge or other public use to promote progress. That's called the power of *eminent domain*. The Constitution recognizes this power and says it is proper for government to have it. But the Fifth Amendment prohibits government from taking a person's property for public use without paying for it at a fair price.

Above: In 2006, John Revelli displayed photographs of the Revelli Tire Company, his family owned business that dates back to 1949, near the construction that took place at the store's former location in downtown Oakland, California. Earlier that year, the city of Oakland used eminent domain to bulldoze the business, which Revelli's father started, to make way for an upscale residential development. The bitter experience led Revelli to join a property rights advocacy group, which urged the state of California to limit the use of eminent domain.

The most controversial Supreme Court decision concerning eminent domain came out of the 2005 case of *Kelo v. New London*. It started five years earlier when the city of New London, Connecticut, made plans to bulldoze all the houses and shops in a rundown neighborhood along the Thames River. The city wanted to do this to make way for a brand new resort hotel and business center. However, the city did not plan to use government workers to build and operate the hotel. The plan was to take the land away from the homeowners and merchants and then hand it over to a private company. The private company would then construct the hotel and be responsible for running it.

Owners of 100 of the neighborhood homes and shops accepted the money offered by the city for their properties. But 15 owners refused to leave. One of them was Susette Kelo. She owned a small house right on the shores of the river. Kelo and the 14 others sued in court to prevent New London from using eminent domain to make them leave their homes. They argued that the way New London wanted to use eminent domain was unconstitutional. They said giving private land to a private company could not be considered a public use.

The Supreme Court disagreed with Kelo. The Court said it *was* a public use because the hotel and business center would result in many jobs being created. That alone would be a big benefit to the community, the Court said. Also, the new buildings and jobs would bring to the city vastly more tax income than the old rundown houses and shops ever possibly could. More tax income would allow the city to better serve the needs of the public, the Court found. Therefore, this particular use of eminent domain was fully constitutional.

Facing page: Bryon Athenian stands on a section of sidewalk that is part of a new development encroaching on his home in New London, Connecticut, February 9, 2005. His dog Charlie walks in the foreground. In 2005 New London won a Supreme Court case allowing the city to force residents from their homes so that a private company could develop the land. The Supreme Court decision was very controversial.

Fairness Will Always Be Important

Many people around the country thought the Supreme Court's decision in *Kelo v. New London* was wrong. They felt it was wrong because it seemed like such an unfair thing for government to be able to take one private person's property and give it to another private person.

But, right or wrong, fairness is indeed at the center of the *Kelo* case, just as fairness is at the center of everything about the entire Fifth Amendment of the Constitution. Fairness is something that is very important to most Americans. It always has been. It always will be.

The United States is not a perfect country. But it is a good country. It is a good country in part because it values fairness. And it values fairness so much that it has made fairness among the highest laws of the land.

It is important to remember that you have a right to fairness just because you were born. It is also important to remember that your right to fairness is not absolute. There are times when the government's need to protect the American people outweighs any one individual's right to fairness. Fortunately, those times are few. And they are few because the Constitution says that the government can only limit an individual's right to fairness when it has a really, really good reason for it.

Above: Fairness is at the center of the Fifth Amendment to the U.S. Constitution.

GLOSSARY

AMENDMENT

When it was created, the Constitution wasn't perfect. The Founding Fathers wisely added a special section. It allowed the Constitution to be changed by future generations. This makes the Constitution flexible. It is able to bend to the will of the people it governs. Changes to the Constitution are called amendments. The first 10 amendments are called the Bill of Rights. An amendment must be approved by two-thirds of both houses of Congress. Once that happens, the amendment must be approved by three-fourths of the states. Then it becomes law. This is a very difficult thing to do. The framers of the Constitution didn't want it changed unless there was a good reason. There have been over 9,000 amendments proposed. Only 27 of them have been ratified, or made into law. Some amendments changed the way our government works. The Twelfth Amendment changed the way we elect our president. The Twenty-Second Amendment limits a president to two terms in office. Constitutional amendments have also increased the freedoms of our citizens. The Thirteenth Amendment finally got rid of slavery. And the Nineteenth Amendment gave women the right to vote.

DICTATORSHIP

A country with a single leader who rules with total power. Citizens of a dictatorship have little or no say in how their country is run. Dictators usually gain their position, and keep their powers, through the use of military force. The Constitution was written to avoid dictatorships. It splits government into three distinct parts: the presidency, Congress, and the Supreme Court. This separation of power keeps any one individual from becoming a dictator.

FOUNDING FATHERS

The men who participated in the Constitutional Convention in 1787, especially the ones who signed the Constitution. Some of the Founding Fathers included George Washington, Benjamin Franklin, John Rutledge, Gouverneur Morris, Alexander Hamilton, and James Madison.

HIGH COURT

Another name for the United States Supreme Court.

INDICTMENT

A formal charge of a serious crime. An indictment is handed down by a grand jury, which decides whether there is enough evidence against a suspect to proceed with a trial.

LAWSUIT

A legal way to settle a dispute in which both sides argue their case in front of a judge or jury in a court of law. The person who has been wronged is called the plaintiff. The person being sued is called the defendant. Plaintiffs and defendants can be individuals, or they can be businesses or government entities, such as corporations or towns. People can even sue the United States, which is how many cases are filed involving the Constitution and violation of rights.

PETIT JURY

A group usually consisting of between 9 and 12 people who meet in a courtroom to decide on the guilt or innocence of individuals accused of a crime. Petit juries are usually the kind seen in courtroom dramas on TV or in the movies.

RATIFICATION

The process of making a proposed law or treaty officially valid. Constitutional amendments are ratified when they are approved by two-thirds of both houses of Congress, and by three-fourths of the states.

SUE

To bring a lawsuit against a person or institution in a court of law.

SUPREME COURT

The United States Supreme Court is the highest court in the country. There are nine judges on the Supreme Court. They make sure local, state, and federal governments are following the rules spelled out in the United States Constitution. Our understanding of the Constitution evolves over time. It is up to the Supreme Court to decide how the Constitution is applied to today's society. When the Supreme Court rules on a case, other courts in the country must follow the decision in similar situations. In this way, the laws of the Constitution are applied equally to all Americans.

INDEX

The U.S. Supreme Court building in Washington, D.C.